This book belongs to

. . . .

Retold by Ronne Randall
Illustrated by Anna C. Leplar

This is a Parragon Publishing Book
First published in 2005

Parragon Publishing
Queen Street House
4 Queen Street
Bath BA1 1HE, UK

ISBN 1-40544-794-X
Printed in Indonesia

The Grimm Brothers

Snow White
and the
Seven Dwarfs

p

One day, as snowflakes fell, a queen sat sewing by her window. Suddenly the needle pricked her finger, and three drops of blood fell onto the snow.

Gazing at the red blood on the white snow, the queen sighed, "I wish I had a child as white as snow, as red as blood, and as black as the wood of the window frame."

Months later, the queen gave birth to a beautiful little girl, who had skin as white as snow, cheeks as red as blood, and hair as black as ebony wood. She was called Snow White.

Sadly, the queen soon died. The king married again, and the new queen was beautiful but vain. Every day she stood before her magic mirror and asked:

"Mirror, mirror, on the wall,
Who is the fairest one of all?"

The mirror always replied:

"You, oh Queen, are fairest of all!"

But little Snow White grew more lovely with each passing year. At last the day came when the queen's magic mirror said:

*"You, oh Queen,
are fair, it's true.
But Snow White is
now fairer than you!"*

The queen was filled with jealous anger.

"No one can be more beautiful than I am!" she snarled.

8

The queen summoned her huntsman.

"Take Snow White into the forest and kill her," said the wicked queen. "Bring me her heart in this chest."

So the huntsman took Snow White deep into the forest. He drew out his knife. But when he looked at Snow White he could not do it.

The huntsman killed a wild pig, put its heart in the chest, and returned to the castle. The wicked queen was pleased, for she was sure that Snow White was dead.

Lost and alone, Snow White stumbled through the dark forest until she came to a little cottage. She knocked at the door, but there was no answer. She tried the latch—the door was unlocked, so she walked in.

Inside, she found a little table set with seven little plates of food and seven little cups of juice. Snow White was hungry and thirsty. So she took a tiny bite from each plate and a tiny sip from each cup.

Soon, Snow White felt sleepy. She climbed the little ladder to the loft and found seven cozy little beds. She lay down on one of them and fell fast asleep.

The cottage belonged to seven dwarfs who worked in the gold mines. Imagine their surprise when they came home to find a stranger asleep in the cottage. And imagine Snow White's surprise when she awoke to find seven pairs of eyes staring at her!

When Snow White told the dwarfs her story, they felt sorry for her.

"If you cook and clean for us," they said, "you can stay here and we will look after you."

The next day, the dwarfs went to work in the mines. Snow White cooked and cleaned in the little cottage.

But back at the castle, the wicked queen was looking in her magic mirror. This time the mirror said:

"Snow White is as lovely as
she is good,
And she lives with the dwarfs,
deep in the wood!"

The queen was furious. She decided to kill Snow White herself. So she dressed up as a peddler woman, and went to the dwarfs' cottage with a basket of ribbons.

"Pretty ribbons to buy!" she called.

Snow White saw the old peddler woman and invited her into the cottage.

"Let me lace your dress with a pretty ribbon," said the peddler woman. And she threaded a blue ribbon through Snow White's dress. Then she pulled it so tight that Snow White could not breathe, and she fell down as if dead.

When the dwarfs came home that evening, they found Snow White lying pale and still on the floor. But when they untied the bodice lace, she began to breathe and her cheeks grew rosy once more.

"The queen will stop at nothing to hurt you," they told her. "You must not let anyone in!"

Snow White promised that she wouldn't.

The next morning, when the dwarfs left for the mine, they made sure that Snow White locked the door. She leaned out of the window to wave goodbye to them.

Back in the castle, the queen went to her magic mirror again. This time the mirror said:

"Fair Snow White, who lives in the wood,
Is still as lovely as she is good!"

Trembling with anger, the wicked queen made a magical potion. With the potion she poisoned a pretty hair comb. Then she set out for the dwarfs' cottage dressed as a poor peasant woman.

"Pretty combs to buy!" she cried.

Snow White opened her window. "I cannot let you in," she said.

"Then come outside and let me comb your beautiful hair," said the peasant woman, showing Snow White a beautiful jeweled comb. Snow White went outside. As the poisoned comb touched Snow White's beautiful black hair, she fell to the floor as if she were dead.

That night, when the dwarfs came home, they found Snow White lying in the cottage garden.

At first they were in despair, but then one of them noticed the comb.

"The evil queen has been up to her nasty tricks again!" said the eldest dwarf, kneeling down to look. Very gently, he took the comb out of Snow White's hair. She soon revived and her pale cheeks grew rosy again.

"The queen will stop at nothing to hurt you," the dwarfs told her. "You must not let anyone in, and you must not go outside!"

Snow White promised that she wouldn't.

The next morning, when the dwarfs left for the mines, they made sure Snow White locked the door, and they kept the key.

This time, when the queen's magic mirror told her that Snow White was still alive, she roared with fury.

The wicked queen made a magical potion. With the potion she poisoned one half of a rosy apple. Then she set off to the dwarfs' cottage dressed as an apple-seller.

"Sweet, rosy apples to buy!" she called outside the window. But Snow White remembered the dwarfs' warning.

"I cannot let you in and I cannot come out," she said.

"Where is the harm in a sweet, rosy apple?" asked the apple-seller. "Look, I will take a bite from this side. It is so sweet and juicy! Taste it for yourself."

Snow White took the poisoned apple. The moment she bit the poisoned apple, she fell down, lifeless.

When the dwarfs found Snow White lying on the floor again, they did everything they could to try to wake her. They loosened her laces, they combed her hair, they washed her face—but she was still and cold.

But the dwarfs did not have the heart to put poor Snow White in a cold grave. Instead, they made her a beautiful casket of glass. They wrote on it in gold letters that she was the daughter of a king.

They set the coffin among the grass and flowers outside their cottage. There they kept watch over her, day and night.

As time passed, Snow White remained as beautiful as ever. She looked as if she were sleeping peacefully in her glass coffin.

One day, a prince came riding through the forest. When he saw Snow White, he instantly fell in love with her. He begged the dwarfs to let him take the casket to his palace.

At first the dwarfs would not agree, but the prince pleaded with them.

"I will love her dearly forever," he promised, and at last the dwarfs agreed.

As the dwarfs lifted the casket, they stumbled. Suddenly a piece of poisoned apple fell from Snow White's mouth, and her eyes opened.

Snow White was alive!

Of course, the moment Snow White set eyes on the prince, she fell in love with him, and when he asked her to marry him, she happily agreed.

Everyone was invited to the wedding, including Snow White's stepmother. But when the wicked queen looked into her magic mirror, it said:

*"You, oh Queen, are fair,
it is true,
But there is one still
fairer than you.
The bride that the prince
will marry tonight
Is none other than the
lovely Snow White!"*

The wicked queen was so enraged that she fell down dead. And Snow White had nothing to fear ever again.

The End